WHAT PEOPLE ARE SAYING ABOUT
THE ADVENT STORYBOOK

There are few things more precious to me than bringing children and families together. *The Advent Storybook* does this in a beautiful, loving, and engaging way as it walks the reader through some of the most important biblical stories to celebrate the greatest gift, Jesus.

BEN COOLEY
CEO, Hope for Justice

Laura and Ian have combined their gifts to share with us a wonderful tool for family discussion. I appreciated the substantive nature of the writing, ripe for meaningful conversation and understanding of the Christmas story. The question posed at the end of each day and the rich illustrations draw the reader and listener into the lesson. Thank you for all this will mean to families during this season!

BETH GUCKENBERGER
Author and Co-Executive Director, Back2Back Ministries

If there was ever a time parents needed help communicating the thread of Christ's coming through the Bible, it is now. Not only will your children have a biblical account of Christmas, but you might just learn a thing or two as well. Extra bonus? The illustrations are simply beautiful!

KELLY KING
Women's Ministry Specialist, LifeWay Christian Resources

Like many, I love Christmas. But I love the true Christmas. The truth of the birth of Christ and the reason for His birth. Laura Richie has demonstrated this truth in her book *The Advent Storybook*. This is a book you will want to read every Christmas season. Your children and grandchildren will pass Laura Richie's project on to their future families.

DR. TED KERSH
President and Bible Teacher, Equipped By His Word

Keeping Scripture fresh in the minds and hearts of my children is a top priority for my wife and me. God's Word has power to go deep in their souls, and Bible stories are the hook that keeps these truths at the forefront of their memories. That's why I love what Laura Richie and Ian Dale have created. Poignant Scriptures, pivotal Bible stories and intriguing illustrations all wrapped up in 25 days of reading makes this book a keeper and the best gift idea of the year.

C.H. DYER
President / CEO, Bright Hope

You will make reading *The Advent Storybook* a treasured part of your family Christmas tradition that will endure for generations. It beautifully and uniquely paints, in words and illustrations, the true story of Christmas—the story of our Rescuer who came from heaven to earth.

JIM GRIFFIN

Vice President, Baptist Medical and Dental Mission International

What an incredible resource for anyone who has or works with children! This is an excellent tool to share WHO Jesus is and the reason WHY He came to earth. I love the clear picture of the Gospel this presents and the HOPE this story brings to us all.

VALERIE SHERRER

Founder, Novo Ministries

Laura Richie has given us a special gift this Christmas season to share with our families. Her collection of Bible vignettes guides us on a journey to discovering God's unfailing plan for His children. Richie's creative recounting of the popular stories culminate in an insightful question to spark deeper conversations with our children. This storybook is a must-have this Advent season for every family.

NORM DUNCAN

Pastor, True Life Church

The Advent Storybook is a beautiful way for families to spend the season of Advent looking at the whole Bible, with Jesus at the center. I love *The Advent Storybook* because it helps us to spend the season of Advent longing and feeling our need for Jesus. Both adults and children will be stirred to come and adore Him.

SEAN EVANS

Pastor, Frontline Church South

Every home should have a copy of *The Advent Storybook*! In the midst of the busy Christmas season, the true meaning of our celebration can slip by unnoticed. Author Laura Richie beautifully engages all ages as she paints the picture of our need for a Rescuer. Your children will eagerly anticipate these daily stories. I know *The Advent Storybook* will become a Christmas tradition for your family.

LAURA SHOOK

Co-Founding Pastor, Community of Faith

The Advent STORYBOOK

25

*Bible Stories
Showing Why
Jesus Came*

Laura Richie

Illustrated by Ian Dale

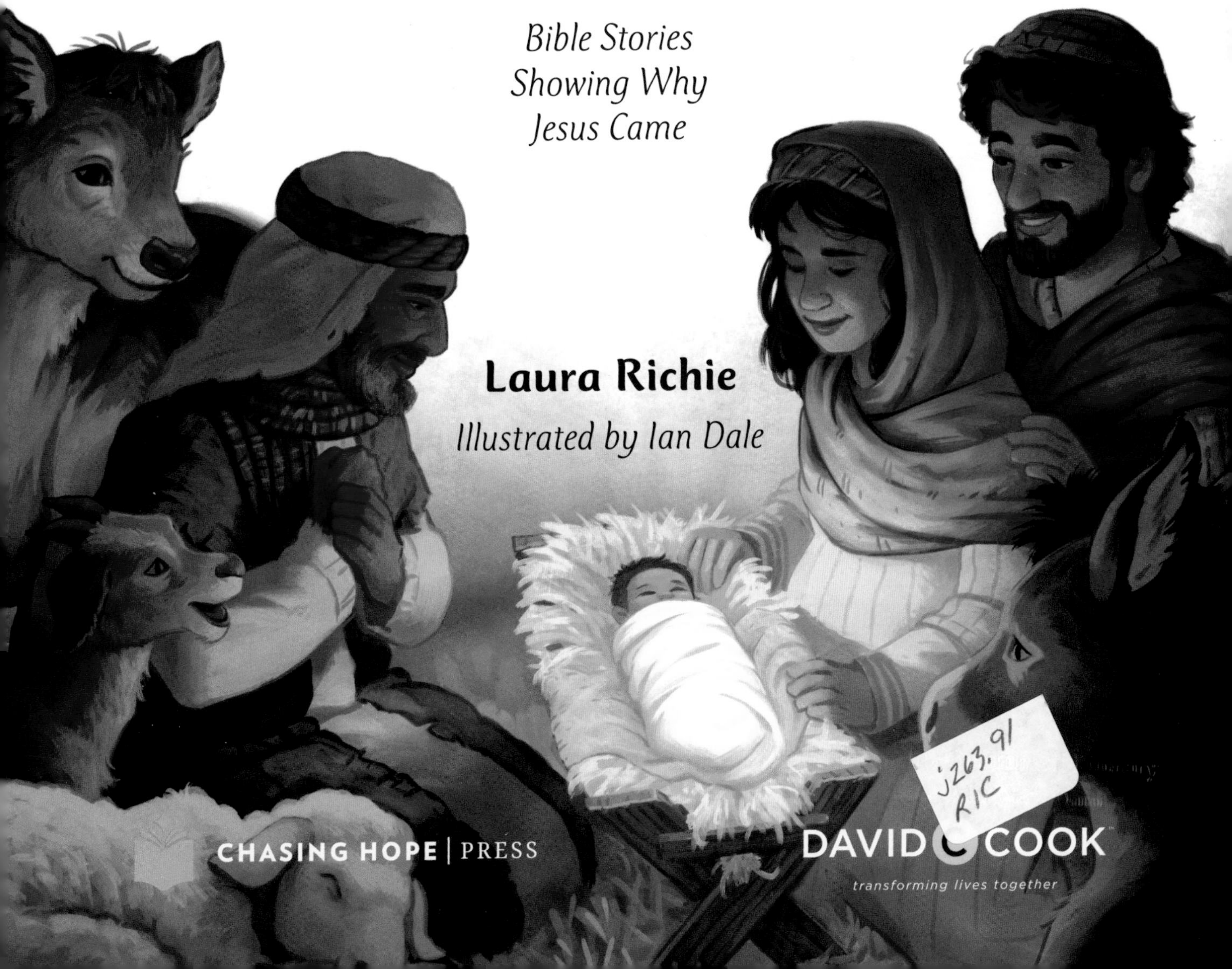

CHASING HOPE | PRESS

DAVID C COOK
transforming lives together

THE ADVENT STORYBOOK
Published by David C Cook
4050 Lee Vance Drive
Colorado Springs, CO 80918 U.S.A.

Integrity Music Limited, a Division of David C Cook
Eastbourne, East Sussex BN23 6NT, England

The graphic circle C logo is a registered trademark of David C Cook.

LCCN 2018938845
ISBN 978-0-8307-7608-5
eISBN 978-0-8307-7713-6

© 2018 Laura Richie
Published in partnership with Chasing Hope Press
Illustrations © 2018 Ian Dale
Designed by Ian Dale

Printed in the United States of America
First Edition 2018

2 3 4 5 6 7 8 9 10 11

101618

CONTENTS

To my sweet family:
Matt, Josiah, Grace, and Isaiah.
May we always remember.
—Laura

To Mandy and Eva,
precious in God's sight and mine.
—Ian

FROM THE AUTHOR

Dear Reader,

The Advent Storybook grew out of my need to remember why Jesus came. We celebrate His birth every Christmas, but I found myself forgetting *why* His coming actually matters. I wrote this to remember, so that my family and I could then truly celebrate the birth of our Rescuer.

I want this book to bring families together around the painfully beautiful story of a once-perfect, now-broken world in desperate need of rescue and renewal. That's why Jesus came. He came to fix broken people, broken relationships, and our broken world. He came to make everything good and new again, like it was in the beginning.

Reading one story each day in December, your family will start with Creation and journey through the Old Testament, tracing God's recurring promise to rescue us. The stories will end on Christmas Day, with the long-anticipated arrival of the Promised Son.

Sit down together and remember how *much* we need a Rescuer and how amazing it is that He came for us! Then celebrate the beauty and grace of our exceptionally *good* God!

Blessings,

Laura Richie

Behold my servant, whom I uphold,
    my chosen, in whom my soul delights;
I have put my Spirit upon him;
    he will bring forth justice to the nations.
He will not cry aloud or lift up his voice,
    or make it heard in the street;
a bruised reed he will not break,
    and a faintly burning wick he will not quench;
    he will faithfully bring forth justice.
He will not grow faint or be discouraged
    till he has established justice in the earth;
    and the coastlands wait for his law.

Thus says God, the LORD,
    who created the heavens and stretched them out,
    who spread out the earth and what comes from it,
who gives breath to the people on it
    and spirit to those who walk in it:
"I am the LORD; I have called you in righteousness;
    I will take you by the hand and keep you;
I will give you as a covenant for the people,
    a light for the nations,
    to open the eyes that are blind,
to bring out the prisoners from the dungeon,
    from the prison those who sit in darkness.
I am the LORD; that is my name;
    my glory I give to no other,
    nor my praise to carved idols.
Behold, the former things have come to pass,
    and new things I now declare;
before they spring forth
    I tell you of them."

ISAIAH 42:1-9

Creation

Genesis 1–2

In the beginning was the Word, and the Word was with God,
and the Word was God. He was in the beginning with God. All things were made
through him, and without him was not any thing made that was made.

JOHN 1:1-3

In the beginning, there was nothing—except God. Then God made *everything.* He formed the sky and shaped the earth. But . . . everything was dark. God's Spirit, like a mother bird, hovered close to His creation.

Then, God said the word, "Light." And do you know what happened? Light began to shine! God just spoke, and it happened! And He said the light was good. He made day and night, and that was the first day.

What did He make next? Sky and dry land, so the earth would not be only ocean everywhere. He called the sky and land and ocean good on that second day.

He made more things, and they were all good! Plants and trees full of delicious food. Good! The sun, moon, and stars to shine down. Good! Fish to fill the ocean, and birds to fill the sky. Good and good!

Each day God made something good and new. On the sixth day, He made the animals to live on land. That same day, God made one more creation . . .

This was the best thing of all. He made people—a man and a woman. He made them to know God and enjoy Him. He made them to love and be loved! God loved them, and He told them to have children and take good care of all the wonderful things He had made.

God's creatures had a beautiful home. No one was ever sad, sick, or hurting. And no one ever died. Everything was very good.

In six days God created everything out of nothing, and on the seventh day, He rested and celebrated. He knew that everything was perfect.

. . . .

Is that how the world is now?

A Perfect Life

Genesis 2–3

In him was life, and the life was the light of men.
The light shines in the darkness, and the darkness has not overcome it.
JOHN 1:4-5

Imagine the most beautiful place you've ever seen. Did it have tall, green trees and bright flowers? Did it smell fresh and sweet, like a garden after the rain? Maybe it had warm sunshine with a cool breeze and birds that chirped and sang.

That's the kind of place God made! He planted a beautiful garden and filled it with everything the man and woman would need.

The garden of Eden was perfect! It had rivers with pure water and many trees with delicious food. It also had lots of creatures to play with and learn about. The man's job was to take care of the beautiful garden and all the animals.

God told the man that he could enjoy the whole garden. God said the man could eat from any tree in the garden, except one. That one was called the tree of knowing good and evil. If he ate from that one tree, then he would die.

The man and woman were both created in God's image—God's beauty and goodness were in them. They loved God, and He loved them. They also loved each other. Everything was perfect and beautiful.

But someone didn't like that.

Darkness and evil crept into the garden. The people had a terrible enemy, called Satan, who hated God. And Satan would do whatever he could to hurt what God had made.

. . . .

We were made to love and be loved. What is love? Love is wanting good for someone and then doing that good. Love is meeting the needs of another even at great cost to yourself. How would you describe love?

A Perfect Life Ends

Genesis 2–3

For all have sinned and fall short of the glory of God, and are justified by his grace as a gift, through the redemption that is in Christ Jesus.

ROMANS 3:23-24

Satan took the form of a snake and found the man and the woman. Satan asked, "Did God *really* say that you can't eat from any tree in the garden?"

The woman corrected Satan. "God said if we eat from just this one tree—or even touch it—we will die."

The serpent lied. "You all won't *really* die. If you eat from it, you will be like God, knowing good *and* evil."

The delicious fruit looked good. It could make them wise. Everything God made was good. Why would God keep a good thing from them? The woman decided to disobey God. She picked the fruit and ate some, and she gave some to the man. He ate the fruit too. And then something terrible happened.

Before, they were clothed by God's glory. Now, they felt naked. Before, they knew only good. Now, they knew evil too. Before, they had never been afraid. Now, they felt guilty and terrified. When they heard God walking in the garden, they hid.

The serpent had deceived the woman. The woman and the man had disobeyed God. The perfect relationships between God, His people, and His creation were gone. So, God told the serpent and the woman and the man what would happen.

The snake must crawl on its belly, eating dust. The woman would be hurt by having babies, and the man would rule over her. The man would work very hard to grow food for his family. And God would send them out of His perfect garden.

But God also spoke a promise. One day, a son of woman would crush the head of the serpent. And the evil that Satan had started would end.

God killed an animal and made clothes for Adam and Eve. They left the beautiful garden. Now death, sadness, fear, and evil were part of their world. Their only hope was God's promise.

· ·

What did they hope for?

The Flood

Genesis 5–8

"This is like the days of Noah . . . For the mountains may depart and the hills be removed, but my steadfast love shall not depart from you, and my covenant of peace shall not be removed," says the LORD, who has compassion on you.

ISAIAH 54:9-10

Adam and Eve had children, and their children had children. Everyone hoped that one of these children would be the Promised Son—the one who would crush evil.

Years went by, and people forgot about God's promise to rescue them. Many people even forgot God. They were trapped in darkness—dark thoughts and dark actions. People destroyed themselves and each other and the earth.

God saw that everything people thought and did was evil. He decided to send a flood to cover the whole world. But God would let one family live.

Noah was a son from the line of Adam. He walked with God and listened to Him. God told Noah how to build a huge boat called an ark. Noah's family and each kind of animal could be rescued from the flood in the ark. Noah believed God, and he obeyed God.

Noah built the ark exactly as God commanded. All the animals and Noah's family entered the ark, and God sealed the door.

Then the rain came down and the waters rose higher and higher. All the animals and Noah's family stayed inside for a very long time—months and months! When the waters finally dropped lower and lower, the ark landed on the mountains of Ararat.

The people and animals left the ark. It was a new beginning. Noah made an altar and gave sacrifices to God, thanking Him for His rescue.

God promised that no matter how evil people became, He would never send another flood to destroy everything. God remembered the promise He had made to Adam and Eve. He set a rainbow in the sky to remind us of His promise.

God is making everything new and good again—one day, ALL the bad will end!

. . . .

What is something bad that you wish would end?

Abram and God's Promise
Genesis 11–12, 15

And if you are Christ's, then you are Abraham's offspring,
heirs according to promise.
GALATIANS 3:29

Noah taught his sons about God and the world. His sons had sons and grandsons of their own. One of these grandsons of grandsons was named Abram. God had a special plan for Abram.

One day, God told Abram to leave his home. God promised that Abram would have a family that would become a great nation. "I will bless you and make your name great, so that you will be a blessing. . . in you all the families of the earth shall be blessed" (Genesis 12:2-3).

But what is a *blessing*?

A blessing is a gift of goodness from God, a part of His plan to bring us closer to Him. God promised to bless Abram, and then through Abram, all the families on earth would have that goodness too! That was a *big*, important promise.

Abram tried to believe God's promise. He took his wife and all his possessions and went where God told him to go. But many years passed and still, he and his wife had no children.

God knew Abram was afraid, so He spoke to him again. God told Abram to look up and count all the stars shining in the sky. He told Abram that his family would be as many as the number of stars in the sky.

And Abram stopped feeling afraid and believed God again.

. . . .

Have you ever had to wait a long time for something? What do you do when you are waiting?

A Promise Kept

Genesis 16–18, 21

Abraham, having patiently waited, obtained the promise.
HEBREWS 6:15

Abram kept waiting for God to give him a son. He waited . . . and waited . . . and waited.

After many more years, Abram and his wife Sarai got tired of waiting. In that time, men sometimes had more than one wife. This was not God's plan, but people didn't trust that God's plan would work. Abram and Sarai didn't trust God to keep His promise—His promise to give them a great family. So, Abram had a son with a different wife.

Thirteen years after that, God came and talked to Abram again. When Abram saw God, he fell to the ground. Abram had made mistakes, but God was not angry with him. God reminded Abram of His promise.

God gave Abram a new name: Abraham. *Abraham* means "father of many." God told Abraham that he would have a very, very big family. Nations would come from him. Kings would come from his family.

God also promised that Abraham's family would have their own home, in a place called Canaan. And best of all, God made a special friendship promise that would last forever—a covenant to love Abraham and his family and to be their God.

Abraham had waited so long. Could he trust in God's promise?

God gave Sarai a new name too—He called her Sarah. Sarah and Abraham were very old. They both laughed at the idea of having a child in their old age.

But God kept His promise! A year later, He gave them a son. Even though they had stopped trusting God, He still loved them and gave them good things. They were so happy to have their son, Isaac!

God reminded Abraham and his family again and again of His promise to love them and be their God. And He reminded them that one day a Promised Son would come who would destroy evil and make everything good and new again.

. . . .

What good gifts has God given you and your family?

Sacrifices
Genesis 22

In these sacrifices there is a reminder of sins every year. For it is impossible for the blood of bulls and goats to take away sins. . . . We have been sanctified through the offering of the body of Jesus Christ once for all.
HEBREWS 10:3-4, 10

For Abraham and Isaac, life was very different from how life is for most of us today. Abraham and his family lived in tents and moved a lot. They had many animals. When the animals had grazed enough in one area, the people moved their animals to a new spot. They moved their tents and their families too.

They also had to dig wells so they would have water to drink. They did not have sinks or faucets. They did not have cars, or electricity, or bathrooms.

What they did have was God. But they couldn't see God or talk to Him whenever they wanted. In the Garden of Eden, Adam and Eve had walked and talked with God. But when they disobeyed God, their friendship with God was broken. In the years afterward, people continued to disobey. Sometimes God would talk to people, like He did with Noah and Abraham. People remembered what God had done for them, and told each other about what they knew.

When people disobey God—when they do bad things that hurt other people, or when they don't love God—that is a sin. Sin breaks our friendship with God. Sin breaks our friendships with other people too.

God gave people a way to repair that friendship, to come closer to Him. They had to make sacrifices. A whole and good life—the life of an animal—had to be taken. The animal didn't do anything bad, but a price had to be paid for the evil that people did.

People did bad things every day. They had to kill many animals for the sacrifices. Sin causes death. Sin is why the world is broken and everything dies.

But we don't have to kill animals for sacrifices anymore. And we don't have to be afraid of death. God has given us a new way to make our friendship with Him whole again. He gave us a perfect sacrifice—a price paid for all our sins.

. . . .

Do you know who is the perfect sacrifice?

Abraham and Isaac

Genesis 22

Know then that it is those of faith who are the sons of Abraham.
GALATIANS 3:7

After Isaac's birth, Abraham knew he could trust God to keep His promises, even if they seemed impossible. Abraham loved his son Isaac and was so proud of him. God had promised Abraham that, through Isaac, his family would be too big to count! And God had promised that the whole earth would be blessed through Abraham's family.

Then something very confusing happened.

God told Abraham that Isaac needed to be a sacrifice for Abraham's sin. Not a lamb or a goat or a dove or any other animal. Isaac. His promised son. Abraham had waited so long for this son. Would God really take Isaac?

But Abraham believed that God was good. He trusted God. So, he took Isaac to the place God told him about, called Mount Moriah. Abraham told his servants that he and Isaac would go up the mountain to worship God, then come back down.

As they hiked up the mountain, Isaac asked his dad, "Where is the animal for the sacrifice? We have fire and wood, but no lamb." His father replied that God would provide the lamb that would die for Abraham's sin.

Abraham prepared the altar for the sacrifice, and he made everything ready to kill his only son—the son God had given him. But at the last moment, God stopped Abraham. An angel spoke this message: "Now I know that you fear God, seeing you have not withheld your son, your only son, from me" (Genesis 22:12).

God provided an animal to die in Isaac's place. He promised again that Abraham's family would bless the whole world. Through Abraham's family, God would keep his promise to the first man and woman. A son would come to end all evil and make all things good again. People would have to wait a *long* time for the Promised Son, just as Abraham had waited a long time for Isaac.

. . . .

Have you ever given up something special to you? How did that make you feel?

Jacob's Family

Genesis 27–30, 37, 39

*Whoever loves his brother abides in the light, and in him there is
no cause for stumbling. But whoever hates his brother
is in the darkness and walks in the darkness.*

1 JOHN 2:10-11

When Isaac grew up, he got married and had two sons. God's promise to give Abraham a big family was starting to come true.

But Isaac's family had many problems. His sons fought a lot. His son Jacob tricked his other son Esau and stole from him. Esau grew so angry that Jacob had to run away.

One night, God gave Jacob the same promises that He had given Abraham and Isaac. Jacob would have a huge family that would bless the whole world!

But Jacob's new family also had problems. Marriage was supposed to be between one man and one woman, like it was at the beginning with Adam and Eve. But Jacob married four women! They fought a lot, because each wife wanted Jacob to love her the best. Jacob soon had twelve sons, and guess what his sons did? They fought a lot too!

They fought the most with one son named Joseph. Jacob loved Joseph the most and gave him special gifts, which made Jacob's other sons very jealous and angry.

Joseph also had dreams that showed his older brothers bowing down to him. Joseph told his brothers about the dreams, and they got so angry that they wanted to kill Joseph! When Joseph was just seventeen years old, his brothers trapped him and sold him as a slave.

How would God's promise to Abraham come true like this? How could a family that fought so much be a blessing to the whole world?

. . . .

What do you think God was planning for Joseph?

Joseph's Trials
Genesis 39–41

*He will swallow up death forever; and the LORD GOD will wipe away tears
from all faces, and the reproach of his people he will take away from all the earth,
for the LORD has spoken. It will be said on that day, "Behold, this is our God;
we have waited for him, that he might save us."*
ISAIAH 25:8-9

Joseph was sold as a slave to a man named Potiphar in Egypt. God helped Joseph so that Potiphar made him the most important worker in his house. But Potiphar's wife told a lie that made Potiphar angry, so he put Joseph in prison.

But God was still with Joseph, and God helped him in everything he did. The man in charge of the prison trusted Joseph and made him a leader in the prison.

Joseph met two prisoners who had worked for the king of Egypt, who was called Pharaoh. Both men had strange dreams. God helped Joseph understand these dreams, and Joseph explained the dreams to the men. And everything came true, just as Joseph had said.

One man went back to work as cupbearer for Pharaoh. Joseph had asked the man to tell Pharaoh about him, but the man forgot.

Two years later, Pharaoh had strange dreams. In the first dream, he saw seven fat cows get eaten by seven skinny, sick cows. Next, he saw seven healthy plants get eaten by seven dried-up plants. No one could explain these dreams to Pharaoh. Then the cupbearer finally remembered Joseph and told Pharaoh about him.

Pharaoh told Joseph the dreams, and God helped Joseph understand them. Egypt would have seven years to grow lots of food. But after that, seven years of famine would come, when no one could grow enough food.

Pharaoh chose a wise man to prepare his country for the famine—Joseph!

God used all the sad things in Joseph's life to make him a very important leader. God was with Joseph through all his trials. And now God was going to use Joseph as part of His promise to bless the whole world!

. . . .

When have you seen God change a bad thing into something good?

Joseph's Brothers

Genesis 41–46

Whoever loves has been born of God and knows God. . . .
In this the love of God was made manifest among us, that God sent
his only Son into the world, so that we might live through him.

1 JOHN 4:7,9

Pharaoh made Joseph the leader in charge of saving food in Egypt during the seven good years. Joseph stored up so much grain that it could not be measured! During that time, Joseph married, and he had two sons.

Then the seven years of famine came. The famine was bad everywhere, not just in Egypt. Joseph's brothers and his father, Jacob, didn't have enough food for their families. Jacob sent his sons to Egypt to get food, but he kept his youngest son, Benjamin, at home.

Joseph saw his brothers come to buy food, but they didn't recognize him. Then they bowed down to Joseph, just like in his dream from long ago.

Joseph had every reason to be angry with his brothers. Because of them, he had suffered as a slave and as a prisoner. When his brothers came to Egypt, Joseph pretended his brothers were spies and put them in prison. Three days later, Joseph released all his brothers but one, Simeon. He gave them food for their families and told them to come back to Egypt with their youngest brother. Otherwise, Simeon would stay in prison.

Joseph's brothers returned with Benjamin, and Joseph cried at the sight of his little brother. Then Joseph told them who he really was. Joseph forgave his brothers for all the evil they had done. He gave them food and a place to live. He loved them.

Later, Joseph told his brothers, "You meant evil against me, but God meant it for good, to bring it about that many people should be kept alive, as they are today" (Genesis 50:20). God had a good purpose even for the bad things that happened to Joseph!

. . . .

Why do you think Joseph forgave and rescued his brothers, even though they had done bad things? Have you ever forgiven someone?

Slavery in Egypt

Exodus 1–3

For freedom Christ has set us free; stand firm therefore,
and do not submit again to a yoke of slavery.
GALATIANS 5:1

Jacob's family moved to Egypt and had plenty to eat during the famine because of Joseph. There were seventy people in Jacob's family at this time. They were called the people of Israel, or Israelites. Abraham and Jacob's family kept growing and growing, just as God had promised!

After Joseph grew old and died, a new Pharaoh ruled Egypt who did not remember Joseph. He saw how big the family of Jacob, or Israel, had become, and he was scared of them. He made them slaves. The Israelites, also called Hebrews, had to work very hard building cities and growing food.

This new king of Egypt was so evil that he told the Hebrew midwives, who helped deliver the new babies, to only allow girl babies to live. But the Hebrew midwives listened to God instead of the evil king. They let the baby boys live too.

During this time, an Israelite woman had a baby boy. She hid him for three months. Then she made a special, waterproof basket for him and put it on the Nile River. The baby's sister, Miriam, watched the basket float. Pharaoh's own daughter found the basket with the crying baby boy inside. She adopted him and named him Moses.

Moses grew up in the palace of Pharaoh, but he knew he was an Israelite. He became angry about the way the Egyptians treated the Israelite slaves. Then Moses made a big mistake. He killed an Egyptian who was hurting a slave. Pharaoh became very angry with him, so Moses ran away to a place called Midian and lived there as a shepherd.

In Egypt, the Israelites cried out to God, asking Him to rescue them from slavery. God heard their cries. And He was going to send a Rescuer.

Just as the Israelites were slaves to the Egyptians, all people are slaves to sin. We all need God to rescue us.

. . . .

What does it mean to be a slave? What does it mean to be free?

Moses and the Plagues

Exodus 4–11

*"The Egyptians shall know that I am the LORD, when I stretch out
my hand against Egypt and bring out the people of Israel from among them."*
EXODUS 7:5

One day, after many years had passed, Moses was watching his sheep in Midian when he saw a bush on fire—but it wasn't burning up! When Moses came close, God spoke from the bush: He wanted to save His people from slavery and give them a good home. God promised to be with Moses, but Moses was afraid. Moses asked God to tell him His name.

God said, "I AM WHO I AM." God told Moses that He would do amazing miracles in Egypt. The Egyptians worshipped pretend gods. They didn't know the one true God. God wanted everyone to know that *He* was the only God.

Moses returned to Egypt to tell Pharaoh to let God's people go. But Pharaoh refused to listen. So, God helped Moses and his brother, Aaron, show Pharaoh a sign of God's power. God turned the water of the Nile River into blood. No one could drink the water, and the fish died. But Pharaoh's heart remained hard.

Then God sent great troubles, called plagues, on Pharaoh's country. Egypt was filled with frogs, then gnats, then flies. But Pharaoh's heart was still hard, so God sent a disease that killed many animals. Pharaoh still wouldn't listen! God made sores appear on animals and people. Then God sent hail and lightning and thunderstorms and swarms of locusts. And God sent a darkness that covered the whole land.

No matter how God showed His power, Pharaoh hardened his heart and would not listen to Moses. He would not let the Israelites go.

God told Moses that He would send one last plague. This one would be the worst. Again, Pharaoh would not listen. At midnight, the firstborn of *every* Egyptian family died. This time, Pharaoh's heart softened. Finally, he let God's people go.

Pharaoh is not the only one with a hard heart. When we are slaves to sin, our hearts become hard too. We need a Rescuer to give us new hearts and set us free.

. . . .

Why do you think Pharaoh didn't want to listen to Moses? Have you ever not wanted to listen to someone who was trying to teach you something?

Passover and Rescue

Exodus 12–15

*I will take you from the nations and gather you from all the countries
and bring you into your own land.*

EZEKIEL 36:24

On the night when every firstborn child and animal in Egypt died, called Passover, God saved the Israelites. God commanded each family to pick a perfect, one-year-old male lamb. They had to kill the lamb and spread the blood on their front doorway. God would *pass over* the houses protected with blood, and everyone inside would be rescued.

At midnight, a great cry arose in Egypt, because someone died in every house that was not covered with blood. Pharaoh's hard heart was broken. He told Moses and Aaron to leave Egypt with all the Israelites and go worship God.

The people left right away. There were now many people in Jacob's family—600,000 men, plus women and children. God told Moses that every year, the people of Israel must remember and celebrate the Passover, because "with a strong hand the Lord has brought you out of Egypt" (Exodus 13:9b).

God was with his people, leading them out of slavery and into the land that would be their new home. During the day, God looked like a pillar of cloud that they could follow. At night, God looked like a pillar of fire that gave them light.

Pharaoh's heart became hard again. He took his whole army and chased after the Israelites, all the way to the Red Sea. The Israelites were very afraid. But Moses told the people, "Fear not, stand firm, and see the salvation of the Lord" (14:13a).

Moses lifted his staff over the sea, as God told him to do. Then God made a dry path through the sea, with a wall of water on the left and a wall of water on the right. The people walked across the sea on dry land! God saved His people again!

The people saw God's power and believed in Him. One day, far away, God would save His people again, through giving up a firstborn Son to set all people free.

· ·

The Israelites were so afraid, but they trusted God to save them. Have you ever been afraid and trusted God to help you? What happened?

Covenant

Exodus 19–20

I will give you a new heart, and a new spirit I will put within you. And I will remove the heart of stone from your flesh and give you a heart of flesh. And I will put my Spirit within you, and cause you to walk in my statutes and be careful to obey my rules.

EZEKIEL 36:26-27

God led His people through the wilderness to Mount Sinai. God wanted to keep a covenant, a lasting friendship promise, with all of Israel. He would be their God, and they would be His people.

God said, "Now therefore, if you will indeed obey my voice and keep my covenant, you shall be my treasured possession among all peoples, for all the earth is mine; and you shall be to me a kingdom of priests and a holy nation" (Exodus 19:5-6).

God came down to the mountain. The people of Israel watched as lightning struck, thunder roared, and a thick cloud of smoke covered the mountain. When God came down, the whole mountain trembled and shook.

When the Israelites saw and heard what God was like, they were scared to be near Him. God called Moses up on the mountain and gave him special instructions for how the people should live. We call these the ten commandments.

Love God, not pretend gods. Don't make idols or pretend gods. Respect God's name; don't misuse it. Remember the Sabbath, the day of rest, and keep it holy. Respect your father and mother. Do not murder. Do not commit adultery. Do not steal. Do not lie. Do not envy something that belongs to someone else.

If God's people would live this way, their lives would be full of good things. They would be good friends with God and with other people. They would love each other and God, which is what they were made to do.

But just like Adam and Eve, God's people often disobeyed God's commands. They broke their relationship with God and with people. And the truth is, all of us break our relationships. To live and love as God created us to do, we need God's help. We need Him to rescue us and give us new hearts—hearts that want good for others.

. . . .

How can we follow God's commands?

Ruth

Ruth 1–4

*By your blood you ransomed people for God from every tribe
and language and people and nation.*
REVELATION 5:9b

The Israelites wandered in the wilderness for forty years, until God brought them to the land He had promised them. There they lived and worked and built the nation of Israel. And they worshipped the one true God.

Ruth lived in a country next to Israel, called Moab. She married a man from Israel. The man and his family had left their home in Bethlehem because of a famine.

But when Ruth's husband died, Ruth had to make a hard choice. She could go back to her family and worship the pretend gods they worshipped, or she could go with her husband's mother, Naomi, to Israel. Naomi was poor, and she had nothing to offer. But Ruth loved Naomi and believed in God.

Ruth made her decision. She told Naomi, "Your people shall be my people, and your God my God" (Ruth 1:16). They went to Israel together, to Bethlehem.

Ruth was a foreigner, and the people of Israel did not trust Moabites. There were probably many people who were not kind to her. But a man named Boaz did a kind thing for Ruth and Naomi.

Boaz grew barley and wheat. One day Ruth went to his field to see if his workers had left any grain behind. Boaz learned who she was. He knew she loved Naomi and trusted in God. He told his workers to protect her and leave extra grain for her. He told Ruth she could come to his field and gather grain every day. Because of Boaz, Ruth and Naomi had food when they were hungry!

Later, Ruth asked Boaz to take care of her so she and Naomi would always have what they needed. And Boaz did! He loved Ruth and married her, and they had a son named Obed. Obed became the grandfather of Israel's greatest king, David! Even though Ruth was not an Israelite, she trusted God. And God made her the great-grandmother of a king! From her family line, another son would come—the King of all kings, born as a baby in Bethlehem, just like Obed!

. . . .

Do you know the name of the King of kings, born as a baby in Bethlehem?

Shepherd and King

1 Samuel 16, 17; 2 Samuel 7

The LORD is my shepherd; I shall not want.
PSALM 23:1

David was the great-grandson of Ruth and Boaz. David took care of sheep—he provided food and water for them, kept them safe from other animals, found them if they got lost, and brought them back home.

One day, an important man of God named Samuel visited David's family to choose the next king of Israel. God chose David, the youngest son, to be the next king. The Bible says, "And the Spirit of the LORD rushed upon David from that day forward" (1 Samuel 16:13). God was with David, protecting him and giving him what he needed, just like a shepherd.

Later, the Israelites were fighting against people called the Philistines. One Philistine was a giant named Goliath. He kept saying that he was stronger than God's people, and he wanted to fight. All the Israelites were afraid.

But not David. He knew that God was his shepherd. He knew God would help him win so "that all the earth may know that there is a God in Israel" (17:46).

When Goliath saw David, he laughed. David was so young and little. But David said, "You come to me with a sword and with a spear and with a javelin, but I come to you in the name of the LORD of hosts, the God of the armies of Israel, whom you have defied" (v. 45).

David knew it didn't matter how strong *he* was, because *God* would help and protect him. And God did! Goliath was defeated.

David became king of Israel. He tried to love God and help his people do the same, but he made many mistakes, just like everyone else. But God made a promise to David. God promised, "Your house and your kingdom shall be made sure forever before me. Your throne shall be established forever" (2 Samuel 7:16).

One day another Shepherd and King would come from David's family. This King would rule forever. And this Shepherd would protect us forever.

. . . .

Who protects you and gives you what you need?

Jonah

Jonah 1–4

*I will make you as a light for the nations, that
my salvation may reach to the end of the earth.*

ISAIAH 49:6

Jonah was a prophet, which means God gave Jonah messages to tell others. One day, God told Jonah to tell the people in Nineveh that they were evil and broken.

But Jonah refused. The people in Nineveh had done terrible things! Why should they get to hear God's message? Jonah knew God wanted to save them.

Jonah got on a ship and went in the opposite direction! He tried to run away from God and His plan to rescue the Ninevites.

God sent a storm with huge waves—a storm so big, it almost broke the ship! Everyone on board cried to their gods for help. Jonah told the sailors what to do. The men called out to Jonah's God, then threw Jonah into the sea. The storm stopped immediately, and those sailors believed in the one true God.

God sent a great fish to rescue Jonah from the sea. The fish swallowed him whole! Jonah stayed in the belly of the fish for three days and nights. He prayed to God, and God made the fish put Jonah back on dry land.

Again, God told Jonah to go to Nineveh to say that in forty days, Nineveh would be destroyed. This time, Jonah obeyed. He told the people God's message, and they believed God! They were very sad about their evil. The people of Nineveh called out to God, and He rescued them.

That made Jonah angry. Jonah didn't want good things to happen to bad people. He didn't realize that he was bad, too. He had also disobeyed God and done evil. But God showed Jonah that the grace of God was for everyone. God loves everyone and everything He has made, and He will rescue anyone who wants to be rescued, no matter how selfish or bad they are.

. . . .

Can you think of someone who needs to be rescued from bad things? How could you show that person God's love?

The Suffering Hero
Isaiah 53

The next day he saw Jesus coming toward him, and said,
"Behold, the Lamb of God, who takes away the sin of the world!"
JOHN 1:29

Isaiah was a good prophet. God gave him messages to tell people, and Isaiah obeyed.

One time, God gave him this message for Israel: God is holy—He is all good with no bad—and He wants to live with His people. But people are NOT holy, so they can't be close to God. They need a hero to rescue them, change them, and bring them close to God.

Isaiah told Israel that God's hero wouldn't be like other heroes they'd known.

This hero wouldn't be handsome or have a lot of money. He would be hated and rejected by people. In fact, people would kill Him.

This hero would be hurt and crushed because of all the bad things other people have done. He would be punished for the sins of everyone—to bring peace between the world and God. Through His body's cuts and bruises and pains and aches, people would be healed in their hearts.

This hero would be like a lamb, being prepared to be killed as a sacrifice. The lamb is silent as the weight of its wool is cut off. It submits to the one in charge. This hero would be silent as He was led to His punishment. He would not shout or fight or struggle. He would submit to the One in charge.

The message God gave Isaiah was for the people of Israel. But the hero in the message is our hero, too. We need a hero who is perfect, like a spotless lamb, to be the sacrifice for our sins.

We need a Rescuer to heal our hearts and help us come close to God again, like Adam and Eve were, and to live with Him.

. . . .

What makes someone a hero? Who is your hero?

Promises of Grace

Isaiah 55, 65

*But according to his promise we are waiting for new heavens
and a new earth in which righteousness dwells.*

2 PETER 3:13

Isaiah told the people of Israel that God would rescue them through a hero. The hero would suffer and die in their place. God also gave Isaiah many messages about grace. Grace means being treated by God as good, even though we do bad.

This is one message God gave Isaiah about God's grace: "Come, everyone who thirsts, come to the waters; and he who has no money, come, buy and eat! Come, buy wine and milk without money and without price" (Isaiah 55:1). God said that His grace is like being able to buy everything we need without having any money!

God also had a grace message about the special lasting friendship promises, or covenants, that He made with Abraham, David, and with all of Israel. No one had kept their side of the promise with God. Everyone had disobeyed. But God still told His people that He would make "an everlasting covenant" with them (Isaiah 55:3).

God knew that people would always break their promises, but He promised to always keep *His* covenant anyway. That is grace!

God gave Isaiah an amazing promise. "For behold, I create new heavens and a new earth, and the former things shall not be remembered or come into mind" (Isaiah 65:17). Everything that is sad and broken and evil will be gone forever, and God will make everything good again! No one will cry or be scared. No one will go hungry or die. All of creation will be made new.

"The wolf and the lamb shall graze together; the lion shall eat straw like the ox, and dust shall be the serpent's food. They shall not hurt or destroy in all my holy mountain" (Isaiah 65:25). Even the animals will be made new and will no longer eat or hurt each other. One day, all creation will be friends with each other and with God, just like in the beginning. And it will all happen through the grace of God!

. . . .

What will the new earth be like?

Josiah
2 Kings 22–23

*"If my people who are called by my name humble themselves,
and pray and seek my face and turn from their wicked ways, then I will
hear from heaven and will forgive their sin and heal their land."*
2 CHRONICLES 7:14

After King David died, other kings ruled God's people. Many of those kings didn't love God. But a few of the kings did good. One was named Josiah.

Josiah was only eight years old when he became king. At that time, most of God's people worshipped pretend gods and had forgotten God's promises. Both his father and grandfather did evil things. But Josiah was different. "He did what was right in the eyes of the Lord and walked in all the way of David his father, and he did not turn aside to the right or to the left" (2 Kings 22:2). Someone had taught Josiah who God was. Josiah decided to follow God and do good rather than evil.

When he was older, Josiah told the people to repair the Temple, the building where people went to be close to God. While they were fixing the Temple, a man named Hilkiah found the Book of the Law. Inside this book were all the stories of what had happened between God and His people, the Israelites.

When King Josiah heard the words of this book, he was so sad that he tore his clothes and cried. Josiah knew that he and his people had done evil. Josiah repented, which means that he wanted to stop doing bad and start doing good instead.

Josiah gathered all the people and read to them from the Book of the Law. And Josiah made a covenant, a lasting friendship promise, with God. When Josiah promised to follow God and obey Him, all the people joined in the promise.

Then, King Josiah celebrated the Passover with all the people. They remembered how the lamb died instead of them, bringing them close, and how God rescued them out of slavery. God helped both Josiah and His people repent and realize their need to be rescued.

. . . .

What does it mean to repent?

Daniel and the Kingdom
Daniel 1–2

*The kingdom of the world has become the kingdom of our Lord
and of his Christ, and he shall reign forever and ever.*
REVELATION 11:15

God loved His people and wanted to be friends with them, but over and over again they stopped loving God.

People from a different country called Babylon fought with Israel. They forced the Israelites to leave the home God had given them. But God still loved His people. He had a plan to bring His people back to Him—not just people from Israel, but people from all over the world!

The king of Babylon chose the smartest and strongest young men to serve at his palace. One of these Israelite men was Daniel. Daniel was determined to follow God no matter what, and God helped Daniel. God gave him wisdom and helped him understand dreams.

The king, named Nebuchadnezzar, had a scary dream. None of the wise men knew what the dream meant. But God showed Daniel the dream.

In his dream, Nebuchadnezzar saw a statue. It had a gold head, silver chest and arms, bronze middle and thighs, iron legs, and feet made from a mixture of clay and iron. A stone struck the image on its feet, and the whole statue fell over in pieces. But the stone that hit the statue became a great mountain that filled the whole earth.

Daniel told the king that the statue showed different kingdoms. His kingdom, the gold head, would end, and other kingdoms would follow. But they would all be wiped away by the stone. The stone represented the kingdom that God would make—one that would last forever and be greater than any kingdom ever was.

After hearing this the king said, "Truly, your God is God of gods and Lord of kings, and a revealer of mysteries, for you have been able to reveal this mystery" (Daniel 2:47).

. . . .

The Promised Son would be the King of this new kingdom of God. What do you think the kingdom of God is like?

Humbled Kings
Daniel 3–6

He has scattered the proud in the thoughts of their hearts; he has brought down the mighty from their thrones and exalted those of humble estate.
LUKE 1:51-52

Daniel was in Babylon many years and served many proud kings. Daniel saw God humble each of these kings to remind everyone that God is the true King.

Once, King Nebuchadnezzar made a statue of himself. He demanded that everyone bow down and worship it. If they didn't, they would be killed with fire. Three of Daniel's friends refused. They said, "Our God whom we serve is able to deliver us from the burning fiery furnace, and he will deliver us out of your hand. But if not, be it known to you, O king, that we will not serve your gods or worship the golden image that you have set up" (Daniel 3:17-18). The king was furious. The three men were thrown into the fire. But God saved them! The king was amazed at God.

Daniel also served King Belshazzar. Belshazzar used special cups from God's Temple to praise his own pretend gods. Then fingers appeared and wrote a message on the palace wall. No one could read the writing, except Daniel. God's message said that Belshazzar's kingdom would end, because he was not worthy. And that very night, the king was killed. His throne was given to Darius the Mede.

Darius put Daniel in charge of the whole kingdom. The other leaders were jealous. So, they tricked the king into making a law against praying to anyone except King Darius. They knew Daniel wouldn't stop praying to God. He prayed three times a day. The king did not want to punish Daniel. When Daniel was thrown into the lions' den, King Darius told him, "May your God, whom you serve continually, deliver you!" (Daniel 6:16).

King Darius didn't sleep at all that night. At dawn, Darius rushed to the lions' den. Daniel was not harmed! God had shut the lions' mouths! Then King Darius wrote a royal law that said, "In all my royal dominion people are to tremble and fear before the God of Daniel, for he is the living God, enduring forever; his kingdom shall never be destroyed, and his dominion shall be to the end" (Daniel 6:26).

. . . .

How is the King of kings different from these kings?

Gabriel's Good News

Luke 1

In the wilderness prepare the way of the LORD;
make straight in the desert a highway for our God.
ISAIAH 40:3

For many years God's people waited for the Promised Son to come and rescue them. Finally, it was time! God sent His angel Gabriel to share the good news.

Zechariah was a priest who worked in God's Temple. Gabriel found Zechariah and told him that God would give his wife, Elizabeth, a son. Zechariah and Elizabeth were too old to have children, but nothing is impossible with God!

This son would be named John. The angel said he would be "filled with the Holy Spirit, even from his mother's womb. And he will turn many of the children of Israel to the Lord their God" (Luke 1:15-16). John would try to help people see their brokenness so they would want the Rescuer's help.

Gabriel also appeared to a young, unmarried woman named Mary. Mary was scared. But the angel said, "Do not be afraid, Mary, for you have found favor with God. And behold, you will conceive in your womb and bear a son, and you shall call his name Jesus. He will be great and will be called the Son of the Most High. And the Lord God will give to him the throne of his father David, and he will reign over the house of Jacob forever, and of his kingdom there will be no end" (vv. 30-33).

Mary's baby would be King forever, just like God had told Daniel! Mary would be the mother of the Promised Son!

Mary knew that many people would not believe her. She could even be killed if she was pregnant but not married. But she believed God and His angel Gabriel—and she wanted the Promised Son to come and rescue them!

While Mary was pregnant, she went to visit Elizabeth, her relative. And the baby John leaped inside Elizabeth's body! He was already full of the Holy Spirit and full of joy, because the Promised Son, Jesus, was growing inside Mary.

Soon, the Rescuer would be born!

. . . .

What is the good news that the angel shared with Zechariah and Mary?

The Promised Son
Matthew 1–2, Luke 1–2

*And the angel answered her, "The Holy Spirit will come upon you,
and the power of the Most High will overshadow you; therefore the
child to be born will be called holy—the Son of God."*
LUKE 1:35

When it was almost time for Jesus to be born, Joseph and Mary had to travel to Joseph's hometown, Bethlehem. It was a long journey, so they stayed with relatives.

At this time, the houses of common people had only one room, and their animals would come inside at night to keep the house warm. Some houses had extra room for guests, but the house of Joseph's relatives was already full. So, Mary and Joseph stayed in the same room as their hosts and the animals.

And in that home, Jesus was born! The Son that God had promised so long ago—the Rescuer, the forever King—was born in the house of common, poor people. He was wrapped in swaddling cloths like any other baby. And He was placed in the animals' manger, their feeding box, to sleep.

That same night, some shepherds were outside watching their sheep. Shepherds were poor and unschooled. Many people didn't like them. But God sent a very important message to these not-so-important people.

God's angel came to the shepherds and said, "I bring you good news of great joy that will be for all the people. For unto you is born this day in the city of David a Savior, who is Christ the Lord" (Luke 2:10-11).

Suddenly a great number of angels appeared! Their glory and light filled the dark night. They were all praising God and saying, "Glory to God in the highest, and on earth peace among those with whom he is pleased!" (Luke 2:14).

The Son that God promised long ago was finally here!

The shepherds were afraid, but they listened to the angel and found Jesus, a baby born in a common house and wrapped in common cloth. And they knew that God had sent this Rescuer for them too. The shepherds praised God!

The shepherds told Mary what the angels had said. Mary looked at her tiny Son. Someday, He would bring peace to this broken world and rescue us all!

Others came to see the new King. Wise, rich men from the East saw a star rise in the sky. They knew it pointed to the King of the Jews, descendants of the Israelites God had rescued long ago. The wise men lived far away, but this King was special—He came to bless all the families of the earth.

They traveled all the way to Bethlehem and found Jesus. When they saw Him, they fell down and worshipped Him. They brought the King of kings expensive gifts of gold, frankincense, and myrrh.

The Promised Son came to rescue all people—Israelite or not, rich or not. Jesus came to bring joy, hope, and peace. He came to be our sacrifice, to die in our place for our sin. He came to be our King—to defeat evil and death, and make everyone and everything good and new again!

....

Come and see the Promised Son!

Who did Jesus come to rescue?

Epilogue

And the scroll of the prophet Isaiah was given to [Jesus]. He unrolled the scroll and found the place where it was written,

"The Spirit of the Lord is upon me,
>   because he has anointed me
>   to proclaim good news to the poor.
He has sent me to proclaim liberty to the captives
>   and recovering of sight to the blind,
>   to set at liberty those who are oppressed,
to proclaim the year of the Lord's favor."

And he rolled up the scroll and gave it back to the attendant and sat down. And the eyes of all in the synagogue were fixed on him. And he began to say to them, "Today this Scripture has been fulfilled in your hearing."

LUKE 4:17-21

ACKNOWLEDGMENTS

So many people have been a part of bringing this book to life:

My husband, Matt, patiently read each version and employed his gentle critique and editing skills to make it more succinct.

My editor, Laura Derico, read the words of a first-time author and (miraculously) saw value in them. She clarified, shortened, and sharpened the stories into their current quality. *The Advent Storybook* would not have happened without her advocacy and expertise.

My illustrator, Ian Dale, created incredible illustrations that share the story of our rescue more clearly than my words. He possesses an uncanny ability at depicting faces and relationships. The first time I saw his illustrations, I knew he was the artist for my book! Ian had just met Chris Scotti, who knew Laura Derico, who connected us to David C Cook. And look where we are today!

All 120 of our Kickstarter supporters believed in my dream and gave generously in order to make it happen.

These people, in particular, gave sacrificially toward the book:

LeRoy & Arnell Griffin   Becky Rogers   Laura Shook   Hovey Yu

Jim Griffin – *To my beloved Janna, wife of my youth, mother,*
grandmother, and woman of God. Proverbs 31:10-29

Kim Lyon – *To my dad, who not only told me about Jesus*
but showed me Jesus by example.

The wisdom of my favorite theologian and New Testament scholar, Dr. Kenneth Bailey, has informed several of these stories, but especially the very last. His influence will be seen even more in the upcoming sequel, *The Easter Storybook*.

God has moved some mountains in order to bring this book to life. Against all odds, I have the privilege of sharing the story of His beauty and rescue! I love Him. Because of His grace, I no longer strive unceasingly to be good enough. Now, I am free to dance in His Light, Life, and Love. To Him be the glory, forever and ever.

ABOUT THE CREATORS

Laura Richie is a wife, homeschooling mom, and registered nurse. A missionary kid for several years, Laura confesses she didn't truly understand her need to be rescued until later in life. Now she delights in sharing the beauty and grace of her Rescuer. Laura resides in Oklahoma with her husband and three children.

Ian Dale is an illustrator and designer who loves to invest in projects that share the hope and meaning that have transformed his life. He has created art for clients such as World Vision, the American Bible Society, Compassion International, and the *Bible App for Kids*, which has been enjoyed in more than 30 languages. Ian and his wife are raising their young daughter in Los Angeles, California. Visit him online at *iandale.net*.

....

Read about the life of Jesus in:

As a family, discover who this Promised Son really was and remember why He had to die. Then celebrate His victorious rescue and return to life on Easter!